Preventing War
A Civilian Effort

By

David K. Ewen, M.Ed.

The first edition of the Ambassador's Journal series

ISBN: 9781072227007
Imprint: Springfield Embassy

Published by Springfield Embassy, a division of New Resurrection Center of Springfield, Inc.

During John F. Kennedy's 1961 presidential inauguration, he said: *"Ask not what your country can do for you – ask what you can do for your country."* This had challenged all Americans to contribute in some way to the public good. That was on Friday, January 20, 1961. The work of Ambassador's in the *civilian sector* for industry does just that and more. With advances in the technology of the internet and associated connected devices, civilians have an opportunity to affect change in ways not possible before. Using business enterprise as a conduit of communication through education, entrepreneurship, and technology support, there is an opportunity to take President Kennedy's challenge to a global level supporting American interests. Of course, this is more advanced than what was proposed in 1961, but we are in a new era of global communication where country boundaries are clouded with international efforts. The International space station is the easiest example, I use to describe this.

International entrepreneurs' part of a small business is increasingly being called upon to serve as a subject matter expert bringing global efforts to greater success by crossing political boundaries that stamp out racial bias and religious

American entrepreneurs have the luxury of freedom that allows them to work internationally and therefore be effective in developing a culture that tears down walls of political confrontation, religious bias, and racial discrimination. We are at a stage of human evolution that we can begin that. There is an opportunity to impact and change the course of our history in a positive way creating a positive legacy for our future to stand on. We can make it better and do more for humanity. The advancement of today's technology allows us to begin that today. There is no good reason not to.

discrimination. They have the character and integrity trusted in the international community offering the opportunity to take on the responsibility of smoothing tensions between nations while at the same time being part of the evolution of the global economy. That is far different and more advanced than the original challenge of president John F. Kennedy in 1961.

By going around political issues that foster the fires of bias and discrimination and self-interest, civilian efforts can create the bridge creating cooperation among nations. success has already been shown in entrepreneurship, education, and technology. These categories best support the interest in smoothing tension among nations.

War is caused by fear. It can be the fear of losing something or not getting enough of something. That something can be essentials like food, energy, and safety. There are other conflicts that are extremist based created by fear.

Governments have traditionally been responsible for the action or inaction related to war. It doesn't have to be that way. President John F. Kennedy said so in 1961 when he said, "*Ask not what your country can do for you – ask what you can do for your country.*"

The advancement of today's technology and those of which are to come to allow civilians to do more in the area of fostering a culture of cooperation and collaboration among nations. The tools are there now and are being used. It is up to civilians to take on the responsibility to help develop that culture of cooperation and collaboration among nations. government officials approach the issue with a political bias for good reason, but it is political bias. Civilians do not have that distraction an obstacle and therefore have an opportunity for success at the same level as government officials.

When people hear the word ambassador, they usually think of a government official representing a country toward another country. Other types of ambassadors are fictitious and represent an organization to a community.

An evolving recognized ambassadorship is growing, showing the interest of a country to represent industries globally. This is in the civilian sector in industry.

The work of an ambassador in the civilian sector for industry is very rewarding, but also offers sacrifices requiring a commitment to meet the obligations that are part of responsibilities supporting global communication across multiple cultures that cross national borders. You do not see limousines and private Learjet being traveled by these types of ambassadors. The income is not so grand as it's not funded by American taxpayers but rather the foreign nations that they support through business enterprise efforts. Simply said, it's not about the ambassador. It's all about the people they support. That is why it is not a job. It is an obligation with responsibilities that go far beyond what would be considered expected by traditional workforce requirements. This is more of a calling to accept the sacrifice. There is a cost associated with a sacrifice that ambassador's take on to fill the needs of the international community in the civilian sector supporting business to improve global communication. Ambassadors in the civilian sector supporting industry are not selfish people. Their humbleness is evident in the communication necessary to cross cultures going beyond national borders.

The distribution of tasks of an ambassador in the civilian sector for industry is done online as there is no separation of countries. This uses the **TOCA** entrepreneurial global business model developed by Ewen Prime Company & Forest Academy. **T** = represents technology such as Internet connection at the foreign destination. **O** = represents operations for client scheduling. **C** = represents client acquisition to build a customer base on foreign lands. **A** = represents audit for legal compliance.

Social media is not a conduit for ambassadors in the civilian sector for industry because the culture of social media is not fitting to the work of an ambassador. You won't see much in the way of ambassadors of this nature in social media. It is more likely that you would see them on Amazon and Barnes & Noble in the form of books and other multimedia content distributed via mass-market online. The books are available wherever books are sold, and consumers can ask for them at any bookstore. Other content stream on mobile devices or seen on television. My office holds this as our platform for content distribution.

More notably, the types of ambassadors that we're talking about are likely to use bridge portals to jump into a virtual shared environment working with clients in a culture of professionalism that is quite different from the casual culture of social media. We call this AVR Jumping when an Ambassador uses VPN, Proxy servers, and other gateway cloud sources to jump IP blocked firewalls to enter countries online.   AVR means Augmented Virtual Reality as the presence from one location to another over great distances is slowly becoming more real as if to bring destinations closer. Today's internet technology and connected devices are growing in quantity and quality, resulting as a preferred method of global contact when multiple countries and continents are involved at a lower cost.

Although the launch of an ambassadorship in the civilian sector for industry is business driven, it is **not** much like being a business owner or having a job. It is not a job. It is an obligation and responsibility that is relevant to global communication in an age of technology that is driven by the next generation of developing leaders of the future.

As part of the culture in a global community of blended countries across industries the work effort and the work ethic go far beyond what one would normally expect from a hardworking workforce. Due to the scheduling of a blended culture associated with their religion and economy, it is quite common for an ambassador to workday and night, seven days a week. Although this lifestyle appears to be that of a workaholic, it is the lifestyle of one being obedient to the obligations and responsibilities of being an ambassador in the civilian sector for industry.   It's not for everyone. Accepting   this   role   means committing to a higher standard of responsibility   serving   humankind. It's not done for the money.   It's done for the people.

My   office   operates   in   three industries of business consulting, educational training, and technology support in Asia, the Middle East, Russia, Europe, and Australia. Our initial   launch   was   in   India   in December of 2013. I had no idea what this venture would evolve into, but   the   sacrifice   has   been rewarding.

I refer to sacrifice in terms of the obligations and responsibilities of an ambassador in the civilian sector for industry area it is quite common to support the Sunday through Thursday schedule while supporting the hard work ethics of Asia working on Saturday and Sunday. The Middle East (Saudi Arabia, etc.) have Friday and Saturday as a weekend and Sunday through Thursday as the business week.

Some people have been confused that the role of an ambassador in the civilian sector can afford to take a day or two off or to take the weekend off without consequences. Quite simply, that is not true. It is a common mistake due to not being aware. The truth is that a contract violation resulting in penalties up to including termination of contract can result because the client can always find someone else. There is a constant flux of new ambassadors entering this new developing workforce while at the same time others leave and give up because of the rigorous requirements. Those that survive the rigors of responsibility understand the gravity and relevance of the obligations to take on this role. It is these people that recognize that the office of ambassadorship in the civilian sector is not to be taken lightly.

Here in the United States, The White House represents citizens and funded by taxpayer dollars. Ambassadors in the civilian sector for industry represent American ingenuity and are funded by foreign nations. The ambassadors are an extension of the White House going beyond borders in the civilian sector. This kind of ambassadorship is recognized through a business enterprise with American interest thereby being an extension of the White House serving as the face of American ingenuity and present-day culture in a global community of industry. It is a significant responsibility with obligations that go beyond the traditional workforce associated with independent civilian business. The result is a different kind of lifestyle of commitment and service to a global community.

A commitment to civilian ambassadorship representing American ingenuity to foreign nations while maintaining authority and respect requires ongoing personal educational development to keep up with trends in technology and culture. Make no mistake - this is a small task. This is part of an obligation that must be satisfied as part of the responsibility of an ambassador in the civilian sector for in district.

What I've presented so far is a clearer representation between government ambassadorship and civilian ambassadorship. A government ambassadorship represents the political interests of America to for nations while civilian ambassadorship represents American ingenuity to multiple nations across various industries. The geopolitical boundaries associated with a government ambassadorship are simply defined as the country's borders. The boundaries associated with the work of a civilian ambassador have no borders and more importantly cross borders as it relates more to global industry a global communication.

An ambassador in the civilian sector for industry representing American ingenuity crosses borders while being fragile in conversation relating to politics and religion. These two topics are not part of the conversation allowing for a more fruitful development in the areas of global communication and entrepreneurial studies supporting worldwide development. It is using industry as a conduit that allows a civilian ambassador to bring unity of global efforts without the distraction of politics and religion that typically caused conflict.

How does one become an ambassador in the civilian sector for industry? It does not happen as a result of a job posting online or some other listing for employment opportunities. That is because the position and role is not a job. It is a calling that is a result of a developed obligation with associated responsibilities. It happens through many years of experience and subject matters experts from foreign nations calling upon an established respected individual to take on an international service representing a level of expertise in global communication and a particular field of study. Usually, a long-term entrepreneur or seasoned business developer with a global experience fit the requirement necessary to be successful as an ambassador in the civilian sector for industry. It takes a specific character with the right integrity to become an Ambassador to satisfy the responsibilities of this magnitude.

Typically, a specific industry is associated with an ambassador or a few at a broad level. My office supports business startups and entrepreneurial studies, educational training, and technology support associated with artificial intelligence. The areas covered support the goal of participating in developing a global community.

Very often, a civilian ambassador will focus on one industry working with multiple nations with represented industry experts in a field. Our office has chosen to choose three categories that are broad to support long-term adaptability. These broad categories include entrepreneurial studies that include business startups, elementary school education, and adult learning, and general technical Support in the area of machine learning for the development of artificial intelligence used for augmented virtual reality environments. We feel that these areas of influence will be relevant in the long term and thus have put the focus on improving expertise counseling ability.

Because an ambassador will work reaching multiple nations and funded by those nations, it is not likely that they would fly in a private

Learjet galloping across the world. The power of the Internet their continually evolved to greater capability along with the proper state of the art leading edge technology that is currently available in the cloud supports a collaborative and community developed environment. It is typical and most common that an ambassador in the civilian sector for industry works from home. There is no fancy office. There is no parade as being a dignitary arriving on foreign land. It's not about the ambassador. It's about the global community being supported. This is nothing like the political envoy work instituted by government entities. Because it is civilian, it is driven by undying passion.

Imagine an ambassador in the civilian sector working with industry experts for an extended period of time. Just imagine that. You can almost imagine the experience that is accelerated because of the different lenses of culture and experiences that cross borders. This is not a common experience. It goes far beyond what the traditional workforce would develop. This is another reason why this role is not considered a job but rather a calling with responsibility presented by nations seeking the subject matter expert. I believe God has the key to all that is involved.

My office represents American ingenuity in the area of business, education, and technology. the cultural discrimination that is common among nations and even within nations can be eliminated when a culture of unity is enforced using the business enterprise as a conduit for communication. The advantage of the business enterprise allows for a method of communication that restricts cultural bias and religious discrimination. In turn, it develops a culture of trust and respect. The result is rewarding because of the obvious positive outcome. Our office supports elementary education in China that will, in turn, create a future of global entrepreneurs who did not grow up in a world of cultural bias and religious diversity attacks. These children will grow up to be more peaceful because they were exposed to an ambassador in the civilian sector. The same holds true for adults who are new to the idea of working internationally. Many years ago, this was not important. With the advances of technology that includes The Internet and all the connected devices make global communication development and improvement so important to the areas associated with closing and shutting down cultural bias and religious discrimination.

It is very delicate work being an ambassador in the civilian sector for industry. We have, so far, talked about the benefits of reducing cultural bias in religious discrimination, but the job requires the delicate white glove service not to put it risk cultural bias and religious discrimination. This requires discernment in understanding how to recognize appropriate body language and facial expressions that go along with chosen words. All of this must be carefully selected as each culture is different within a single nation, let alone the nation by itself. The aristocrats in cities operate differently than peasants in the countryside. Government officials and dignitaries behave in a way that is different from the general workforce. Experienced international travelers will have a different level of understanding of business than a small business owner serving local customers. It is quite common for the kind of ambassador we are talking about to work closely with a wide variety of cultures and different walks of life within a country. And every country is different. More importantly, the trends change, and so there is a constant learning process, and that is part of the sacrifice that an ambassador makes when taking on this obligation with multiple responsibilities.

As technology evolves on the foundation of the Internet and associated connected devices and in an ever growing and more powerful wireless network, the nation's borders will grow to become more clouded requiring more ambassadors in the civilian sector to support industry allowing for improved global communication that is above racial bias and religious discrimination. With strong effort and a long road ahead, the ambassadors of the next generation can make it possible for all nations to work together.   It almost sounds easy, but the truth is that with every advance, there is a setback that serves as a foundation for the next advance resulting in the slow motion forward to the desired goal. It will be difficult. That is why the job of an ambassador is a sacrifice with obligations to be met through responsibilities.

No one learns to walk in the shoes of an ambassador in the civilian sector supporting industry. There are many who believe they know, but don't due to ignorance resulting from a lack of experience. Years ago, I was ignorant too, not knowing. Even those who initially become an ambassador think they know what the calling is and what the responsibility is all about. They don't. I know that, because I didn't when I started. It's not possible to know in advance what the future holds. There is nothing that prepares you for an ever-changing world with unexpected events that changed the course of history and therefore how to avoid the tragedies of racial bias add religious discrimination while at the same time improving global communication to steer away from those tragedies. That's what an ambassador in the civilian sector for industry works with.

It's a huge undertaking to accept ambassadorship that can't be prepared for in advance. All the years of knowledge building, experiences, and evolved wisdom are merged together with good character and trusted integrity to make an ambassador who can make the right strategic decisions and choose the most eloquent words. It takes a long time to cook up an ambassador who is fearless and ambitious to serve people in a global community. The seed begins with a profession and the flower is the calling held at a higher standard.

The Bible teaches us that there are consequences for our actions resulting from the decisions we make. These consequences were demonstrated thousands of years ago and we still see the same kind of consequences today. The human race is fragile as demonstrated by this history, but we have multiplied and evolved so more help is needed. With god's help and guidance and encouragement, the ambassador in the civilian sector for industry can use the language of business and entrepreneurial studies to improve global communication to help the human race continued to grow as it has been but preferably even better.

One of the responsibilities that an ambassador has is to put the world in a better place than when they found it. That's a huge responsibility. It's an obligation that's hard to accept. That is why it's called a sacrifice. And ambassador has the challenge to guide nations at the civilian level into a culture that forgets racial bias and religious discrimination.   As the expression goes … easier said than done.

The seven pillars of the Models of Excellence serve as a resource developed by Ewen Prime Company and Forest Academy for Ambassadors in the civilian sector for Industry. It serves as the foundation for ambassadors to start their work.

After a time, the work ambassadors do takes on its' own life. No one is the same. The wisdom from experiences that drive the decisions and motivations of each ambassador could never be alike with another. That is why so many ambassadors in the civilian sector are needed. The global community can benefit from this blend of wisdom.

The seven pillars of the Models of Excellence include motivation, organization, discipline, ethics, learning, strength, and combinations of the previous six pillars. The Models of Excellence is the engine providing a mechanism of growth among nations working cooperatively. Teamwork is built using the tools suggested for an ambassador to the nations in the civilian sector for industry. This is how we prevent wars. It sounds simple, but the implementation crosses borders best satisfied by the services of an ambassador. Resources and ideas are shared and fairly distributed rather than being fought over. This is just one way we can prevent wars. It's not the only way, but one that is very important. It's foundational and is the seed for other strategies.

There are seven pillars representing the Models of Excellence. They are the following:

(1) Motivation
(2) Organization
(3) Discipline
(4) Ethics
(5) Learning
(6) Strength
(7) Combination

The seventh pillar, "Combination" is a combination of the previous six pillars. Each can stand alone and combined with others.

Motivation

The first pillar called motivation is the get up and go attitude that is self-driven offering a reason for acting and behaving in a beneficial way. Motivation is void of a state of Slumber and laziness.

It is easy to be in a state of slumber and behave in a lazy way. It requires fortitude and perseverance to be motivated. This requires a desired focused attention to be void of a lazy behavior. This action is self-driven and not controlled or swayed by others. Motivation is a responsibility that is based on action.

We all have choices in life. The choice to accept and embrace motivation is ours alone. We can choose to accept it or deny it. Accepting it has rewards. Denying it has consequences. The choice determines the outcome of rewards or consequences.

In Proverbs 6:9 the scripture reads, "How long will you slumber, O sluggard? When will you rise from your sleep?

Organization

Having organization put structure in life so that there is a path toward an objective allowing for the reward of a goal to be achieved. Without organization, there is no road map to a goal because no goal exists. Those who have organization accomplish things that are beneficial to themselves and others. Without organization. There is miss-direction and a sense of unawareness. The result is a confusing state of mind. By having organization, there is understanding, assured behavior, incompetent awareness. This allows accomplishments and goals to be achieved.

In 1st Corinthians 14:40, the scripture reads, "Let all things be done decently and in order."

In Luke 14:28, the scripture reads, "For which of you, intending to build a tower, does not sit down first and count the cost, whether he has enough to finish it"

<u>Discipline</u>

Discipline is knowing the difference between what you must do compared to what you want to do. Sometimes what you want to do interferes with what you must do. Doing what you must do will never negatively impact what you want to do. Discipline is understanding priorities in life by recognizing what must be done. There is an understanding of consequences when priorities are not met. That understanding insurance that consequences are avoided resulting in priorities taking precedence in our lives. Discipline requires obedience to the focused attention of the priorities that must be done. It involves a constant awareness and action to fulfill priorities as necessary.

In Hebrews 12:11, the scripture reads, "Now no chastening seems to be joyful for the present, but painful; nevertheless, afterward it yields the peaceable fruit of righteousness to those who have been trained by it."

In Titus 1:8, the scripture reads, "but hospitable, a lover of what is good, sober-minded, just, holy, self-controlled,"

Ethics

Ethics is knowing the difference between right and wrong. By not having ethics, wrong can be committed without being aware that it is not right. There is a firm division between what is considered right and what is considered wrong. One way that is created is by the legal system. A more important way is what is inherently understood and expected within Humanity. The actions of people, when honorable and respectful, tend to lean toward what is right and steer away from what is wrong.

In Luke 6:31, the scripture reads, "And just as you want men to do to you, you also do to them likewise."

In Matthew 7:12, the scripture reads, "Therefore, whatever you want men to do to you, do also to them, for this is the Law and the Prophets."

Learning

The process of learning never ends, and we can all receive edification from others. By being mindful and respectful to the understanding that learning never ends we can achieve greater wisdom beyond the knowledge of which it is founded. Education not only comes from schools, but also from experiences, conversation, suffering through consequences, achieving successes, and sharing with others. There are so many avenues of learning and edification that an open mind can receive and continue to grow beyond expectations and to greater awareness.

In Proverbs 1:5 the scripture reads, "A wise man will hear and increase learning, and a man of understanding will attain wise counsel,"

In Luke 6:40, the scripture reads, "A disciple is not above his teacher, but everyone who is perfectly trained will be like his teacher."

<u>Strength</u>

Strength represents not giving up. It is the endurance to continue even when difficult times are ahead. With strength, the adversities in life will not be a hindrance to reaching goals and becoming successful. Being void of strength allows any obstacle to prevent moving forward to any success resulting in total absolute failure. To avoid failure, strength is necessary to endure and overcome obstacles put in our path. Strength is also represented by self-control to persevere and continue forth through storms in life. When considering strength needed in life consider the words endurance and self-control.

In Colossians 1:11, the scripture reads, "strengthened with all might, according to His glorious power, for all patience and longsuffering with joy;"

In Philippians 4:13, the scripture reads, "I can do all things through Christ who strengthens me."

<u>Combination</u>

The seventh and final pillar representing models of Excellence is a combination of the previous six. For example, to be organized you must be disciplined. To have ethics you must learn what is right and wrong. To have motivation, you must have strength

One of the reasons there are seven pillars representing the models of Excellence is that the number 7 has significance. In the Book of Genesis, God created the heavens and the Earth and rested on the 7th Day. The number 7 represent something being finished or complete. Thereafter, in the Bible, the number 7 represented define perfection or completion.

In no way does the Seven Pillars representing the models of Excellence replace or make less of the nine fruits of the spirit as noted in the book of Galatians. In Galatians 5:22-23, the scripture reads, "But the fruit of the Spirit is love, joy, peace, longsuffering, kindness, goodness, faithfulness, gentleness, self-control. Against such there is no law."

<u>Discerning Evil</u>

To maintain models of excellence in our lives there must be a minimal level of distraction. The ability to discern evil ensures that our wrongness found in the world we live in does not deter us from the direction necessary for us to succeed. The evil to be discerned are in the categories of deception, manipulation, and selfishness by others who may make effort to influence us. The recognition of this evil in advance will easily stomp out a possible deception, manipulation, and selfishness that others try to impose upon us.

In 1st John 4:1-3, the scripture reads, "Beloved, do not believe every spirit, but test the spirits to see whether they are from God, for many false prophets have gone out into the world. By this you know the Spirit of God: every spirit that confesses that Jesus Christ has come in the flesh is from God, and every spirit that does not confess Jesus is not from God. This is the spirit of the antichrist, which you heard was coming and now is in the world already."

<u>Deception</u>

In the bible from the book of Proverbs chapter 6 verses 16 to 19 says "There are six things that the Lord hates, seven that are an abomination to him: haughty eyes, a lying tongue, and hands that shed innocent blood, a heart that devises wicked plans, feet that make haste to run to evil, a false witness who breathes out lies, and one who sows discord among brothers. "

In the bible from the book of Revelations chapter 12 verse 9 says "And the great dragon was thrown down, that ancient serpent, who is called the devil and Satan, the deceiver of the whole world—he was thrown down to the earth, and his angels were thrown down with him."

In the bible from the book of first of Timothy chapter 4 verse 1, the scripture reads: Now the Spirit expressly says that in later times some will depart from the faith by devoting themselves to deceitful spirits and teachings of demons,

Different evil behavior is defined as one or more of the characteristics of deception, manipulation, or operating under self-serving behavior. Self-serving behavior is selfishness.

Let us talk about deception and define what it is. Deception is the action of deceiving someone. It is action that results in deceit.

Deception is fraudulent behavior involving trickery, chicanery, slyness. A bluff to give pretense of something else is a form of treachery. This deception has many purposes including manipulation and to satisfy selfishness. Manipulation and selfishness encompass two of the tree axis of evil. Deception is the third. manipulation and selfishness can result from deception. This example shows how deception, manipulation, and selfishness operate together.

The act of deception has the intent of not telling the truth. The truth is hidden. God says that the truth will set you free. With deception, there is no freedom. The difficulty from continual deception has to do with keeping the story straight for long term believability. If the story resulting from deception has no truth, the difficulty of maintaining consistency has difficulties. Fabricating a story with the intent of swaying a person's belief's or actions require continual fabrication to ensure successful deception. The person of deceit does not know how far they must act on deceiving. This behavior fails in the long term, because the discernment of fake behavior cannot last forever.

Manipulation

In the bible from the book of Matthew chapter 7 verse 15, the scripture reads: "Beware of false prophets, who come to you in sheep's clothing but inwardly are ravenous wolves.

In the bible in the book of Matthew chapter 24 verse 4, the scripture reads: And Jesus answered them, "See that no one leads you astray.

In the bible in the book of Hebrews chapter 13 verse 8 to 9, the scripture reads: Jesus Christ is the same yesterday and today and forever. Do not be led away by diverse and strange teachings, for it is good for the heart to be strengthened by grace, not by foods, which have not benefited those devoted to them.

Manipulation involves the skillful handling or controlling something or someone. The purpose of that skillful handling may include selfishness and involves treachery, deception, and a bluff. Once again, we see how deception relates to manipulation and selfishness. The process of manipulation convinces someone to do something or think in a particular way. The method of manipulation involves pressure, force, and an act of urgency. manipulation in no way relates to a polite request unless deception is involved. Deception changes the way others think. Manipulation pushes people to do something that they would not consider themselves. This shows that manipulation has a selfish purpose, as it does not satisfy the needs of the manipulated person or victim of manipulation.

People can be manipulated to do many things. They can be forced by threat or treachery to do something at their own expense. The manipulator saves money by pushing the expense to the one being manipulated. Other forms of manipulation involve creating a benefit to those creating the deceit for selfish reasons. Victims of manipulation receive no reward or benefit. The victims incur a cost either in money, time, property, convenience or emotion. Manipulation creates value or convenience to a selfish deceptive person. The victim loses in the form of some value and level of convenience.

<u>Selfishness</u>

In the bible from the book of Romans 2:8, the scripture reads: But for those who are self-seeking and do not obey the truth, but obey unrighteousness, there will be wrath and fury.

In the bible from the book of first Corinthians chapter 10 verse 24, the scripture reads: Let no one seek his own good, but the good of his neighbor.

In the bible from the book of Romans chapter 12 verse 3, the scripture reads: For by the grace given to me I say to everyone among you not to think of himself more highly than he ought to think, but to think with sober judgment, each according to the measure of faith that God has assigned.

Selfishness is the quality or condition of lacking consideration for others. People who are selfish concern themselves with their own profit or pleasure. Selfish people receive profit or pleasure at the expense of others. This is done by deception and manipulation. Again, we see how deception, manipulation, and selfishness relate to each other.

The best ways to discern selfish behavior is to identify people who carry a high ego. People who are egocentric and egotistical show self-centered behavior identified as selfish. The resulting behavior of selfishness includes being inconsiderate, thoughtless, uncaring, uncharitable, mean, greedy, and opportunistic. This behavior satisfies selfish people with ignorance to victims of selfish behavior.

Deception, Manipulation, and Selfishness

In the bible from the book of Mark chapter 7 verse 21 to 23, the scripture reads: For from within, out of the heart of man, come evil thoughts, sexual immorality, theft, murder, adultery, coveting, wickedness, deceit, sensuality, envy, slander, pride, foolishness. All these evil things come from within, and they defile a person."

In the bible from the book of 1st of John chapter 3 verse 9 says No one born of God makes a practice of sinning, for God's seed abides in him, and he cannot keep on sinning because he has been born of God.

The word evil shares a combination of attributes of deception, manipulation, and Selfishness. Deception requires manipulation and selfishness. Manipulation requires selfishness and deception. Selfishness includes deception and manipulation. All three behaviors related to each other. With the combination of all three behaviors in motion, identifying evil behavior challenges even the more astute and intuitive person.

A way to identify evil tendencies involves breaking up the behaviors of deception, manipulation, and selfishness and identifying each one. When one is identified, then the other two can be identified by relating it to the first identified behavior. For example, an act of deception identified as a behavioral flaw. This flaw in turn relates to manipulation and selfishness. Once all three behaviors show clearly that shows evil. Identifying evil involves first identifying either deception, manipulation, or selfishness. Second, the other two behaviors show relevance to the first behavior identified.

Selfish behavior requires manipulation to deceive someone. The tendency of being selfish results in deceptive manipulation. To deceive through manipulation, require selfish behavior. Just know that evil behavior shares behaviors between deception, manipulation, and selfishness.

<u>Integrity</u>

A person's character is a measurement of their integrity. That character comes from a measurement of evil behavior such as deception, manipulation, and selfishness. As the bible reminds us, we are all born into sin. We have the ability to deceive, manipulate, or have selfish tendencies. We all can improve our character by keeping a watchful eye on our levels of deception, manipulation, and selfishness. By reducing all three behaviors, our integrity greatly improves and shown in our character. You language and behavior speak of your character. The ways you carry yourself and speak to others speak of your character. The more positive the character, the greater a person's integrity is. Keep check on yourself. Take a close look to see, if even to a small innocent degree, if you carry traits of deception, manipulating, or selfishness.

<u>Behavior</u>

Poor behaviors include hypocrisy and condemnation. Hypocrisy is the practice of claiming to have moral standards or beliefs to which one's own behavior does not conform. In other words, hypocrisy is the behavior of a person condemning others for the same behavior that they possess. It is a form of deceptive behavior previously talked about. This behavior can also be used for manipulation. Hypocrisy is for selfish purposes. This means that hypocrisy or being hypocritical falls into evil behavior. People to condemn others when they themselves should share in the condemnation use hypocrisy.

Love

In conclusion, just know that your language and behavior speak to your character which is a measurement of your integrity. Do you want to do better? Look at the scriptures identified in this book and attend a bible-based Christian church. Check within yourself for characteristics of deception, manipulation, and selfishness. If you can capture those three characteristics and hold them harnessed, then you will see improved behavior. Instead, look toward LOVE, as the right behavior.

LOVE = Let Our Voice Encourage

In the bible from first Corinthians chapter 13 verses 4 to 8, it reads: Love is patient and kind; love does not envy or boast; it is not arrogant or rude. It does not insist on its own way; it is not irritable or resentful; it does not rejoice at wrong-doing, but rejoices with the truth. Love bears all things, believes all things, hopes all things, endures all things. Love never ends. As for prophecies, they will pass away; as for tongues, they will cease; as for knowledge, it will pass away.

In the book of John chapter 3 verse16, it says: For God so loved the world, that he gave his only Son, that whoever believes in him should not perish but have eternal life.

From the bible, in the book of Mark chapter 12 verse 31 it says: The second is this: 'You shall love your neighbor as yourself.' There is no other commandment greater than these."

In the bible from the book of Luke chapter 6 verse 35, it says: But love your enemies, and do good, and lend, expecting nothing in return, and your reward will be great, and you will be sons of the Most High, for he is kind to the ungrateful and the evil.

Closing

In closing what has been discussed in this presentation has been related to civilian responsibilities to improve cooperation and collaboration among nations that in turn re strict political borders, racial bias, and religious discrimination. a proposed tool to facilitate this process using ambassadors in the civilian sector for industry are the seven pillars of the Models of Excellence.

We know that our future within humankind is more crowded with diverse cultures that can only succeed in continued growth If a culture of collaboration and cooperation is given. The fostering of this culture falls on the shoulders of ambassadors in the civilian sector for industry using the conduit of business, education, or technology development. Government can provide the political strategies and can do it very well, but that is only what can be offered.

The civilian effort goes beyond political borders and restrictions and satisfies the quest first launched by President John F Kennedy in 1961. that being said, the civilian ambassador working globally carries the responsibility serving as an extension of the White House because they represent the American people in front of the nations. Although a huge responsibility, it must be considered part of our American heritage to not only accept foreign Nationals on

American soil come up but to treat them the same on foreign soil. This is done with honor and respect.

About the author

Amb. David K. Ewen, M.Ed. is an Ambassador to the nations in the civilian sector supporting business startups, entrepreneurs, educational training, and technology support. His work reaches Asia, the Middle East, Russia, Europe, and Australia. David is a former touring professor lecturing on global communication, digital multimedia technology, and entrepreneurial studies. He has been an entrepreneur since 1994 and authored several books that have also been released in audiobook and documentary form.

About the book

Preventing War is a letter to the president of the United States written in June 2019 to acknowledge civilian responsibility to bring nations together in a culture of cooperation and collaboration.

The author is an ambassador to the nations in the civilian sector for industry and offers his seven pillars of the Models of Excellence.